ZOOM IN ON

THE FIRST HUMANS

ADAPTED BY

DOUGLAS PALMER

KING*f*ISHER

Contents

A Story

Lou and the Bear Cub   4

Information

Our First Ancestors   12

A Remarkable Journey   14

Humans and Apes   16

Evolution – what is it ?   18

Origin of the Hominids   20

Lucy and the
    Australopithecines   22

Conquering the Savannah   24

Heading out from Africa   26

Mystery of the Neandertals   28

The Rise of Modern Humans   30

A Game

One day was just like
    another !   3:

Information

Digging up the Past   3·

Anecdotes

Incredible but True !   3·

Information

Stepping Out   38
The Discovery of Fire   40
What Did They Eat ?   42
Living in Groups   44
From Trees to Caves   46

An Activity

The Terra Amata Hut   48

Information

The Hunters and the Hunted   50
Tools and Techniques   52
Rock Art   54

An Activity

Learn to Paint
  Stone Age Style   56

A Test

True or False ?   58 – 61

Index   62

Solution   63

Stickers

Postcards

Lou and the Bear Cub

The cave of the Wolf Clan

I remember well that icy night. Everything that flew, walked or crawled seemed to be frozen in an uneasy silence. The air seemed to crackle and the rocks to moan. At the edge of the cave, my mother stood breathing in air that froze the blood. Suddenly, a block of stone crushed her foot. The cave had collapsed on the sleeping clan.

A Story

My mother had time only to throw me out. "Save yourself, Lou! Get out!"

At some point, I regained consciousness. I ached all over. It was hot. And hairy. Without wishing to boast, I already had a keen sense of smell. Bear! An inert she-bear was crushing me. I wriggled free. A rock had broken her skull. At her side, a bear cub was squealing. I enticed it towards me: "Don't cry, Bear Cub."

I thought of my own family, the Cro-Magnon Clan of the Wolf, and of my mother who was now dead. Bear Cub licked my tears. He snuggled up against me; a warm ball, he brought heat back to me. For several moons we wandered, sharing our solitude, fear, hunger, roots, berries, salmon, bathing and games... until the day our path crossed with the Neandertals of the Clan of the Bear.

Urs the Wise suggested to the clan that they offer me a home. He hoped, I think, to gain favour with the Wind, the Snow and the Cold.

"Welcome to you, Lou Who Commands the Spirit of the Bear!" he proclaimed. "May the fire of the Clan of the Bear protect you from now on."

Urs the Fool protested: "I am against it. Lou is different. She's a Cro-Magnon. The Cro-Magnons occupy our hunting and gathering grounds. They

5

are always pushing us farther away. And you want to save their daughter? Has Urs the Wise gone mad?"

"Like us, Lou is a daughter of the Land of Fire! Look at her playing with my son Urs-Boy. The children have taken to each other. Why should adults choose the path of hatred?"

Many moons later, I would ask myself the same question…

The Great Hunt

"Men are always looking for a quarrel. Why?"

On the day of the Great Hunt, this question of Urs the Wise was on my mind. I had shared the fire of Urs-Boy, in accordance with the wish of Urs the Wise. Urs-Boy was skilful at shaping stones. Together we had learned how to skin a deer and scrape it to remove the fat and flesh before tanning. Without wishing to boast, I often had good ideas.

"Lou," he said to me, "you would be a fine companion if you spent less time with that bear."

"Bear Cub lives his own life, Urs-Boy…"

And we laughed and rolled on the grass.

That morning, Urs-Boy took me hunting. We made a good team. Because of my speed and agility, I waited for the woolly rhino in order to

trap it. I could hear Urs-Boy's cries behind the hill. With a torch, he set fire to the vegetation to drive out the rhino. He drove the rhino towards me. It was then that they suddenly appeared. There were three of them. They blocked my way.

"I am Kerd of the Deer Clan of Neandertals," said the largest of them. "Get out of our way, grasshopper! We have been trailing the woolly rhinoceros for three suns!"

I replied that I was Lou, from the Neandertal Clan of the Bears. And how they laughed! I did not like the way they looked at me.

"I am Krew and I spill the blood of Cro-Magnon grasshoppers like you!" said the biggest one.

"But you will have to catch me first, Krew! I leap about like the flames while you drag yourself along like a worm. Your legs hardly allow you to climb over even the flattest stones!"

The third one threw himself at me roaring, "I am Krak! I will break your bones, insolent grasshopper!"

What could I say? Some people are always trying to pick a fight. Bear Cub had responded to my call of distress. The Clan of the Deer made a bolt for it when they saw him swooping down on

them. Without wishing to boast, I love showing off *our* strength!

"Gently, Bear Cub!"

Bear Cub shook himself against me. He pushed with me with his large head. I laughed. "You are no longer a little hairy ball, but a monster!"

The galloping of a rhino reverberated on the ground. The animal, a large male, appeared straight in front of us. Bear Cub moved away, growling. The rhino saw me and charged. I jumped up, my heart in my mouth. At the last moment, as I felt that dangerous breath upon me, I rolled to the side and the rhino plunged into the ditch we had chosen as a trap. Urs-Boy rejoined me, out of breath but delighted by the success of the hunt. The Clan of the Bear would have meat to preserve in the snow!

"And a beautiful horn!" I added. "Provided that Kerd, Krak and Krew of the Clan of the Deer do not come and try to take the beast from us!"

I told Urs about it. "The Deer Clan should not be so far south," he said. "Unless..."

"Unless what?"

"Unless their hunting territory has dwindled because of the Cro-Magnons."

"I know," I said, bowing my head, "the Cro-Magnons are driving us back by gradually taking over the hunting grounds that we abandon. Urs the Wise explained it to me so that I could understand why Urs the Fool hates me so."

"It is not your fault, Lou. The Cro-Magnons are no longer your people since we adopted you. The Clan of the Bear are proud to count you as one of their own. And I don't think you're too bad, either!"

Urs-Boy laughed as hugged me. I blushed.

"I have won my colours in the fight against the rhino," I said, to divert attention from myself.

"Go," replied Urs-Boy, "it is time to inform the Clan of the Bear that the rhino is waiting for them to kill it. I will stay here and watch over the animal."

Let the Spirit of the Bear receive you, Urs!

When I returned with the Clan of the Bear to the site of our hunt, I was in for a shock. I rushed towards the slope shouting, "Urs! Urs, answer me!"

Urs-Boy, wounded, was lying on the ground close to the hole, with Krew stretched out near him. Krak had fallen into the ditch, where the rhino had trampled him. Kerd had fled.

"I'm pleased to see you again, grasshopper," murmured Urs-Boy.

I stroked his hair; his forehead seemed hot. He

tried to smile, but he was so pale. Blood had made his fur coat sticky. Bear Cub licked it clean. Then the medicine man attended to the wound. Urs the Wise focused his attention on his son, who did not move.

He said: "The Spirit of the Bear has left the body of my child." And when he rose, looking terribly aged, he pointed to the crest of the hill and said: "Let us take the body of brave Urs-Boy. We will leave the woolly rhino."

I was astonished, but I understood the reason for this withdrawal. Some Cro-Magnon men, spread out in a semi-circle, were approaching slowly. They had stone weapons, but did not look aggressive. I guessed they were simply determined to recover the fruit of our hunting. A number of them went past us.

Urs the Fool cried: "Why are we giving way? The Cro-Magnons will drive us to starvation if we do not fight them!"

Urs the Wise eyed Urs the Fool scornfully. There was a silent struggle. Urs the Wise was thinking of the survival of the Neandertal women and children. For how many months?

I withdrew with the others, walking alongside Urs-Boy, who was unconscious on a stretcher.

A Story

"Without you, Urs-Boy," I murmured, taking his hand, "without you, hunting will not be the same. The clan pays homage to your courage. You were a brave hunter. You will travel in the Big Sleep with the skull of a bear and ten ibex horns. I will speak to the Spirit of the Bear in your favour. Bear Cub and I, we will never forget you. I loved you, Urs."

"Can you repeat that?"

Urs-Boy had seized my hand. He smiled at me!

"Urs!" I cried. "Urs the Sly! Don't ever do that again! Never!"

I was confused, frightened, happy!

Did my love have the power to bring back life?

Our First Ancestors, the Hominids

The story of Cro-Magnon Lou and her Neandertal friend Urs-Boy is the most recent chapter in the unfinished tale of the rise of the human species.

▧ The world and the start of life

Scientists think that the Earth was created around 4,500 million years ago and that microscopic life forms first appeared in the oceans about 2,800 million years ago. Another 2,000 million years passed before simple jellyfish-like creatures appeared. And it was a further 795 million years before our ape-like ancestors developed – a mere five million years ago.

Humans

▧ Who are hominids?

All the people of the world are so closely related that we belong to a single species, *Homo sapiens*. Our ancestors were just one of several species of human-like apes who together are called hominids.

Paranthropes

Australopithecines

Information

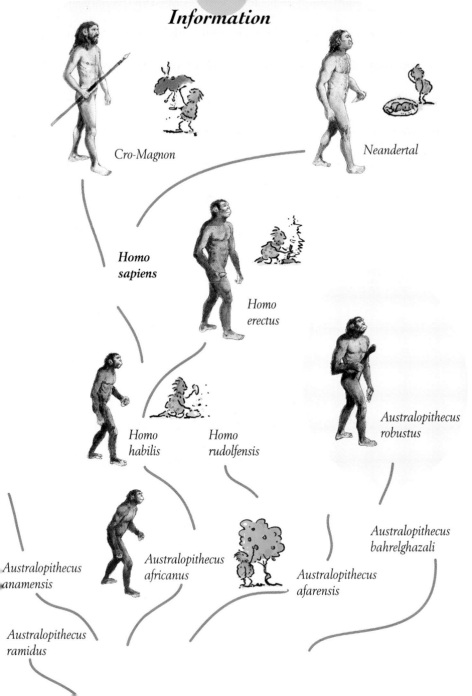

Cro-Magnon

Neandertal

Homo sapiens

Homo erectus

Australopithecus robustus

Homo habilis

Homo rudolfensis

Australopithecus anamensis

Australopithecus africanus

Australopithecus afarensis

Australopithecus bahrelghazali

Australopithecus ramidus

A Remarkabl

Humans, chimps and gorillas share a common ancestor, who lived in the forests of Africa less than ten million years ago.

■ Seven million years ago, as the Earth's climate cooled, our hominid ancestors had to leave the protection of the shrinking forests in east Africa and venture into the wide open grasslands of the savannah.

■ Four million years ago, as they began to walk upright, groups of hominids were able to spread farther and farther throughout central and southern Africa.

■ Two million years ago, the evolving hominids split into several species. Some groups developed stone tools and moved out of Africa as far as Asia.

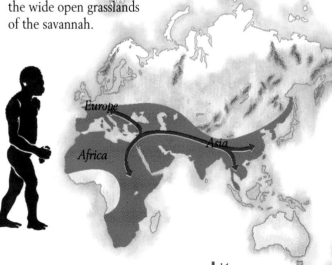

Journey

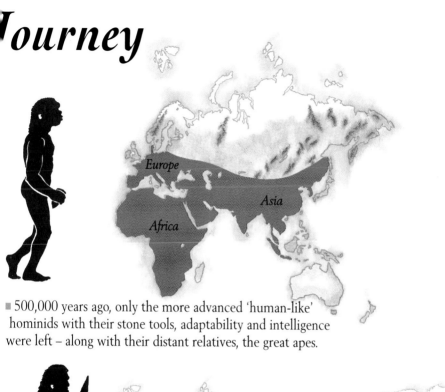

■ 500,000 years ago, only the more advanced 'human-like' hominids with their stone tools, adaptability and intelligence were left – along with their distant relatives, the great apes.

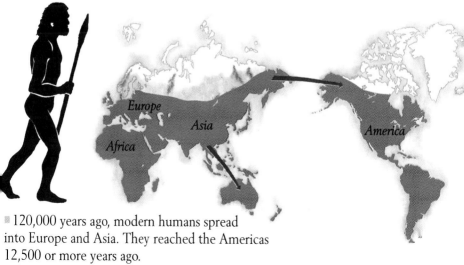

■ 120,000 years ago, modern humans spread into Europe and Asia. They reached the Americas 12,500 or more years ago.

Humans an

Charles Darwin was the first person to put forward the idea, in 1871, that humans are closely related to apes. Until recently, people resented the suggestion.

Genes in every cell of our bodies determine what we are – human ape-like animals. Our genes are responsible for characteristics that we inherit from our parents, and we pass them on to our children.

■ The wrong end of the stick

It is a mistake to think that we are directly descended from apes. We are not, but every bone in the human body is basically the same as those of the apes.

■ Blood relations

Human *genes* and body proteins are similar to those of the apes. Biologically we are so close that the split between human and ape ancestors may have occurred as recently as five million years ago.

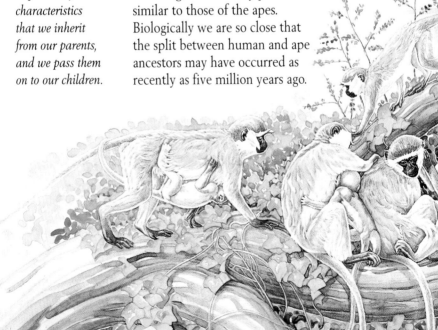

pes

◼ Common behaviour

Humans and the African apes (chimps and gorillas) behave in similar ways. They use tools and weapons, and they work in groups for hunting and defence. They live in family groups, and can live for many years.

◼ A number of common features

Hair, warm blood and milk for their young distinguish mammals from other vertebrates (backboned animals). Large brains, good sight and grasping hands and feet all distinguish the monkeys, apes and humans as primate mammals.

Chimpanzee   *Gorilla*

Evolution — what is it?

Evolution is the changes that take place in animal and plant life over a period of time. These changes produce new species. Some species become extinct, but others evolve and replace them.

■ When the forests die off...

In a drought, trees produce fewer leaves and competition between living creatures for plant food intensifies. When their environment changes like this, living creatures have to adapt – only the toughest species survive. Some of our ape-like ancestors had the advantage of being able to walk upright. So they were better able to survive by moving out onto the open grassland savannah.

■ Survival of the fittest

In each species, including humans, there are some variations. Only those with the most suitable variations for the new conditions can continue to breed. Thanks to their genes, offspring are copies of their parents and inherit the characteristics of the fittest.

■ Survival of the luckiest?

For over 140 million years, between 205 and 65 million years ago, dinosaurs and early mammals lived alongside each other. It was an unequal struggle, dominated by the reptilian dinosaurs. Then bad luck in the form of a giant meteor hit Earth, temperatures dropped, and dinosaurs became extinct. That catastrophe let the surviving mammals take over. The new mammals included the first primates – the early ancestors of monkeys, apes and humans.

Animals have to adapt to changes in the environment. The mountains of this river valley are covered in trees.

If the climate becomes drier, there are fewer trees. The animals have to compete for food and only some survive.

When the climate becomes wetter again the trees return. Sufficient food allows new species to develop.

Origin of the Hominids

The oldest fossils of our hominid ancestors have been found in East Africa. They are over four million years old.

■ The planet of the apes

Rift Valley

Earth really was the planet of the apes 15 million years ago – there were over 30 different species. Very few of these survived, but in Africa one group of chimp-sized apes evolved that was both adept at climbing *and* occasionally walked semi-upright on their hind legs. They were the hominid ancestors of modern apes and humans. The oldest known of these ancestors are the australopithecines.

■ The beginning of human features

The australopithecines lived over four million years ago. Most of their features, such as strong arm bones, are typically ape-like. But they also had a crucial human-like feature in the way the spinal nerve cord was connected to the brain.

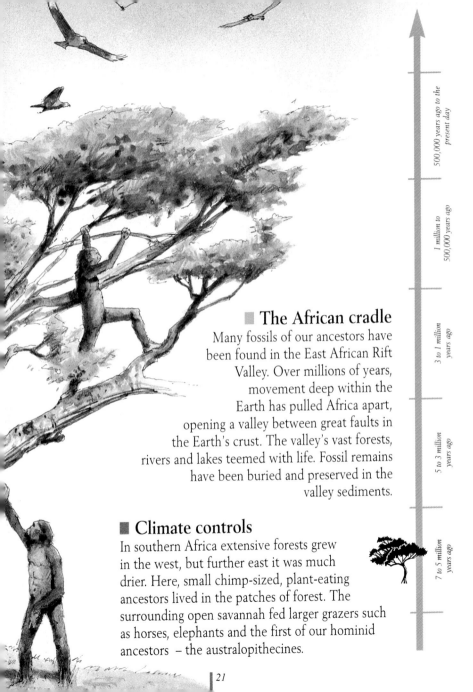

■ The African cradle

Many fossils of our ancestors have been found in the East African Rift Valley. Over millions of years, movement deep within the Earth has pulled Africa apart, opening a valley between great faults in the Earth's crust. The valley's vast forests, rivers and lakes teemed with life. Fossil remains have been buried and preserved in the valley sediments.

■ Climate controls

In southern Africa extensive forests grew in the west, but further east it was much drier. Here, small chimp-sized, plant-eating ancestors lived in the patches of forest. The surrounding open savannah fed larger grazers such as horses, elephants and the first of our hominid ancestors – the australopithecines.

500,000 years ago to the present day

1 million to 500,000 years ago

3 to 1 million years ago

5 to 3 million years ago

7 to 5 million years ago

Lucy and the

Africa was home to the
australopithecines, or 'southern apes',
for more than four million years.

A growing family

Between four and one million years ago, more and more
australopithecines spread throughout Africa, well
beyond the Rift Valley. The more they could walk
upright, instead of *knuckle-walking* like their ape-
ancestors, the more widespread they became. They
evolved into a number of different species.

*Knuckle-
walking uses
the knuckles
as extra feet.*

Large and small

Australopithecines show big differences
in build between the sexes. Males were
about 1.5 m tall and weighed up to 70
kg. Females were shorter and lighter.

Australopithecines

▇ Lucy, an australopithecine teenager

In 1974, the *fossil* skeleton of a young female hominid, was found in Ethiopia. Just over 1 m tall, she weighed 30 kg and was able to walk upright. Nicknamed Lucy and dated at three to four million years old, she is one of the oldest australopithecines known.

▇ A new find

Lucy is known as *Australopithecus afarensis*. In 1995 an even older hominid was found in the Rift Valley and named *Australopithecus anamensis*. This

Fossils are remains found in rocks.

is the oldest known australopithecine (4.2 to 3.9 million years old). Like Lucy, it could walk upright.

▇ Everyday life of an australopithecine

Like apes today, australopithecines probably lived in family groups for protection and gathering food. As the areas of forest became smaller, they moved out into the savannah grasslands. They had to change their feeding habits from gathering fruits and nuts to hunting small game and searching for buried plant food such as roots, tubers and bulbs.

500,000 years ago to the present day

1 million to 500,000 years ago

3 to 1 million years ago

5 to 3 million years ago

7 to 5 million years ago

Conquering the Savannah

Between three and two million years ago, a drier and cooler climate brought big changes in the evolution of the hominids. Woodlands receded and the savannah became more extensive.

■ Clever but not yet human

The advanced australopithecines were heavier and had bigger brains – some may even have made simple stone tools such as hammers and choppers. But they still had ape-like faces, with powerful jaws and large teeth.

■ Human ancestors

Just over two million years ago, new hominids appeared in Africa with significantly larger brains. These were the first primitive humans. Some distinct species have been recognized. 'Handy man', *Homo habilis*, lived 2 to 1.6 million years ago and had hands capable of making stone tools. These human ancestors evolved faster than the australopithecine relatives that survived – the paranthropes and the newly evolved modern apes, chimps and gorillas.

Homo is the Latin word for 'man', and includes all the different human species.

Information

■ Human ancestors

Just over two million years ago, new hominids appeared in Africa with significantly larger brains. These were the first primitive humans. Some distinct species have been recognized. 'Handy man', *Homo habilis*, lived 2 to 1.6 million years ago and had hands capable of making stone tools. These human ancestors evolved faster than their surviving australopithecine relatives – the paranthropes and the newly evolved modern apes, chimps and gorillas.

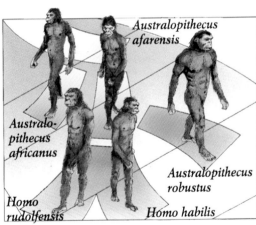

Australopithecus afarensis

Australopithecus africanus

Australopithecus robustus

Homo rudolfensis

Homo habilis

■ The first hand tools

The first stone tools were roughly-shaped rocks. Earlier wooden tools may have existed but have not been preserved. It is not known exactly which hominid group made the stone tools.

500,000 years ago to the present day

1 million to 500,000 years ago

3 to 1 million years ago

5 to 3 million years ago

7 to 5 million years ago

Heading ou

As the global climate cooled, primitive humans packed their tools and headed out of Africa to Europe and Asia.

■ The first large humans

From two million years ago, primitive humans grew taller (up to 1.5 m) and their faces became flatter, with a prominent brow ridge. For the first time, the hominid brain reached a size comparable to that of modern humans.

■ New tools

New stone tools appeared around 1.6 million years ago. They had a rounded handhold and a pointed end with two cutting edges. For over a million years, these simple but skilfully-made hand-axes were the common stone tool.

■ The first schools?

Finds of these two-edged (bifacial) axes are often the only evidence of early human occupation. Their similarity and distribution over Africa, Europe and Asia suggests that the manufacturing technique must have been carefully taught by example and passed from generation to generation.

rom Africa

◼ The first travellers

The first wave of travellers quickly spread well beyond Africa. Hand-axes and the fossil remains of primitive humans known as *Homo erectus* ('upright man') have been found from France to China and Java. The distinctive Acheulian axes are called after the place where they were first found, at St Acheul in France.

◼ Campfires

Arriving in China one million years ago, some *Homo erectus* started living in caves and used fire for the first time. However, there was no fireside chat – these early humans, like apes today, probably had a very limited repertoire of sounds.

500,000 years ago to the present day

1 million year to 500,000 years ago

3 to 1 million years ago

5 to 3 million years ago

7 to 5 million years ago

The Mystery o

Another wave of early humans moving out of Africa produced the tough Neandertals, who could cope with the climate of Ice Age Europe.

Neandertals were named after a fossil skull that was found in the Neander Valley in Germany.

■ The puzzle of the missing link

There is a huge gap between 1.8 and 0.8 million years ago in the story of early humans. No evidence has yet been found to explain the link between *Homo erectus* and the *Neandertals*. About 800,000 years ago, the ancestors of the Neandertals moved out of Africa.

he Neandertals

500,000 years ago
to the present day

1 million to 500,000
years ago

3 to 1 million
years ago

5 to 3 million
years ago

7 to 5 million
years ago

■ The Ice Age survivors

Faced with the Ice Age climate in Europe, the Neandertals had to be tough, intelligent and adaptable survivors. They grew up to 1.7 m tall, weighed up to 76 kg, and had brains as big as, if not bigger than, modern humans. Neandertals might not stand out from the crowd in a cosmopolitan city today. But if you looked closer you would notice a strong brow ridge, a large flat nose and a receding chin.

■ The Neandertal way of life

Neandertals were excellent hunters and tracked migrating animals. But this hard way of life took its toll – they died young, often from hunting injuries. There is evidence that they were the first humans to care for sick relatives, and that they buried their dead.

The first musicians

Part of a Neandertal flute was found in a cave in Croatia. It was made from the hollow thigh bone of a bear. Dated at 43,000 to 67,000 years old, it is the oldest known musical instrument.

The Rise o

The immediate ancestry of modern humans is still uncertain. These tall, well-built Cro-Magnons are the ancestors of all living humans and gradually became the dominant hominids.

Homo sapiens refers to our Cro-Magnon ancestors and us, modern humans.

■ The human family

All living peoples belong to one species, *Homo sapiens* ('thinking man'). We probably originated in Africa, around 100,000 years ago. However, scientists now think that some of our genes also came from an Asian ancestor.

■ Mighty Cro-Magnons

The first modern humans had large brains, like the Neandertals, but were taller (up to 1.8 m). In fact, they were significantly bigger, stronger and brainier than the average human today.

Cro-Magnons used traps, lines and barbed spears to catch fish.

Modern Humans

Throwing an assegai with the help of a propeller

The cultural revolution

Around 50,000 years ago, much more advanced tools like the *assegai* were developed. They were made of bone, wood, sinew and stone, and had finely-worked blades. Instead of caves for shelter, permanent dwellings were constructed from stone, wood or mammoth bones. Pictures of prey were painted and engraved on walls, and ornaments were traded. The dead were buried.

Modern humans take over

Early modern humans lived alongside the Neandertals until about 35,000 years ago, when the Neandertals disappeared. Recent analysis of Neandertal bones suggests that they did not interbreed with the Cro-Magnons and left no descendants.

An assegai was a throwing spear made of wood with an iron tip.

31

One day was just like another!

This scene of daily life is set 30,000 years ago. At first glance, there is nothing particularly strange about it. But look closely and you will see that there are 18 mistakes. See if you can spot them all.

Solution on p. 63

A Game

POST NO BILLS

Digging u

The team:

- *Archaeologists study tools and other objects.*
- *Palaeontologists specialize in non-hominid fossils.*
- *Palaeo-anthropologists work on hominid fossils.*
- *Sedimentologists analyze sediments to reconstruct how and where they were laid down.*
- *Geologists examine rocks to find out how they were formed.*
- *Geochemists analyze the chemistry of rocks and date them.*
- *Palynologists identify fossil pollen to assess the vegetation and climate of the past.*

Excavation

of a prehistoric site is like a criminal investigation. It requires teamwork and an eye for detail – no clue must be missed. This is how we discover the past.

▮ Laying down the past

Wind and water deposit sediment on the ground. As time passes, these deposits form layers that harden and pile up on top of one another. The upper surface is always the most recent. The tools and fossils that were buried in the sediment can be dated by their position in the sequence of layers.

he Past

■ Looking for clues

Even the tiniest fragment of bone, perhaps part of a skull, may be a vital clue in unravelling the history of an archaeological site. A flake of stone could be a tool or a weapon. Charcoal may indicate fire. Even the dirt itself may contain pollen for chemical analysis. Each surface has to be mapped, measured and closely examined for such clues. A team of many different specialists may take weeks, or even years, to piece together the whole picture.

■ Hidden treasures

Understanding prehistory is restricted by a lack of fossils and artefacts. There are still only a few thousand identifiable and datable hominid remains, which come from a few hundred sites worldwide. Even well-known areas, such as the East African Rift Valley, have been only partly searched. And there are no written records – prehistory is pre writing. But as teams of archaeologists from around the world continue their work, new discoveries come to light almost every month.

Incredible but True!

■ A great step forward

In 1976, Mary Leakey discovered a unique set of
footprints at Laetoli, Tanzania. They proved that our
remote ancestors were capable of walking upright at least
3.6 million years ago. The tracks show that two adults
walked side by side and a child followed behind, carefully
stepping in the prints of one of the adults. They were
walking across a soft fresh layer of volcanic ash from one
of the many volcanoes in the East African Rift Valley.
Mary Leakey, her husband Louis and various members of
the next generation, especially Richard, have been
responsible for finding many of the remarkable hominid
fossils from East Africa over the last 50 years.

■ What happened to the Peking hominid fossils?

One of the richest hominid finds outside Africa lay in some hillside caves not far from
Peking (now called Beijing) in 1926. A succession of European and American
archaeologists excavated the site over many years. By the time the Japanese invaded
China during World War II, 40 partial skeletons and six nearly complete skulls had been
collected. The precious fossils were to be sent to America for safe-keeping, but only
one case arrived and it contained plaster casts. No one knows for sure what happened
to the others. One of the best hominid treasures seems to have been lost for all time.

The Taung child

A beautiful, small, ape-like skull with large human-like teeth is one of the most valuable 'missing link' fossils in the human story. But when it was found in 1924, in a limestone quarry in the village of Taung in South Africa, few scientists recognized its importance. Fortunately, the fossil was sent to the anatomist Raymond Dart, of the University of Witswatersrand. He saw that its structure bridged the gap between the skull and teeth of the apes and those of humans. He named it *Australopithecus africanus* – the African southern ape. Another 40 years went by before Dart's diagnosis of this new species was accepted.

A lucky accident

In September 1940, two teenagers accidentally fell into an underground cavern near Montignac in Perigord, France, as they tried to rescue their dog. Little did they suspect what they were going to find. They had stumbled upon a Stone Age cave with walls covered in spectacular images of wild cattle, bison, deer, a woolly rhinoceros and a cave bear. These wonderful, coloured paintings date back 17,000 years.

Stepping

Evidence that hominds were *bipedal*
at least four million years ago comes
from fossil leg joints and footprints.

▊ Legs made for climbing

Although apes can walk in a semi-upright position,
the joints of their leg bones and feet restrict the
movement to a bow-legged waddle, a bit like that
of a human baby. The leg joints of our ape-like
ancestors were better adapted for climbing and
knuckle-walking than
walking upright.

> *Bipedal is
> walking on
> two legs.*

Australopithecine

Homo habilis

)ut

■ Evidence for walking upright

The leg bone of a four-million-year-old African hominid, called *Australopithecus anamensis*, shows that it was the first of our ancestors to walk upright. Fossil footprints at Laetoli in Tanzania confirm its bipedalism. But long arm bones mean it could still climb trees.

■ Legs made for walking

Walking upright requires several changes to the muscles and joints of the legs, especially the connection with the pelvis. Also, the feet need to have long heels and short toes. These changes meant that the legs and feet were no longer so good for climbing. Once hominids walked upright, there was no turning back.

)mo erectus   *Neandertal*   *Cro-Magnon*

The Discovery

Making and using fire was one of the most important skills of the advanced hominids. With fire they could keep warm, cook meat, improve their weapons and protect themselves against predators at night.

Lighting a fire by rubbing a stick

f Fire

■ First find your fire...

Fire is a natural phenomenon, produced by volcanoes or lightning strikes on tinder-dry vegetation. Early hominids probably collected smouldering timber from natural forest fires and discovered burned animal carcasses, or 'roast meat'.

Lighting a fire by striking sparks from flints

■ Using fire

Fire-baked earth in Kenya, around 1.5 million years old, may be the earliest evidence of the use of fire by hominids. In Europe and Asia, hearths found with ash, charcoal layers and blackened bones suggest that cooking was done by early humans around 500,000 years ago. However, it is not known whether the fire was actually made or 'captured' from a natural fire.

■ Making fire

Rubbing sticks together and striking sparks from flints were probably the first means of making fire. Dry leaves and twigs catch fire and burst into flames. These methods are still used by a few remote societies.

What Did They Eat?

Humans are omnivorous and eat many different kinds of food. But our ape-like ancestors mostly ate parts of plants.

■ The first hominids liked to chew

Our early hominid ancestors were plant-eaters and had no fire for preparing their food. Raw plants are low-energy food and herbivores had to spend a lot of time foraging, chewing and digesting. They needed powerful jaws and large teeth to chew tough plant material and make it easier to digest.

Omnivorous means eating both animal and vegetable food.

■ A mixed diet

Meat is a relatively rich source of energy and is easier and quicker to eat. The change to a diet that included raw meat is linked to the bipedal australopithecines who first left the shelter of the African forests around four million years ago.

■ The first cooks

The use of fire had an important effect on the human diet. It meant that meat could be roasted and then preserved by smoking. Some plant products such as tubers and roots could also be baked to remove poisons.

■Food for thought

Our brains make up only
two percent of our body
mass, but they use up
20 percent of our energy.
Perhaps the shift away
from vegetable foods to
high-protein, high-energy
meat diets, prepared by
cooking, is linked to
the increase in
brain size, which
occurred over
600,000 years ago.

*The discovery
of fire meant
that food could
be cooked to
make it easier
to digest.*

Living in Groups

Our hominid ancestors probably lived in small family groups, like the living apes do today. This gave them a number of advantages.

Hunting in groups was less dangerous, and there was a greater chance of success.

Why live together?

Like the living apes, hominids were not particularly strong or fast. Living in open areas exposed them to danger – from predators and from other groups of hominids. Survival depended on sharing a range of talents and using them intelligently. Living together in a group required greater communication and organization. And that meant leadership and rules of behaviour.

The need for speech

Living and working together as a group, or society, may have stimulated the development of human speech.

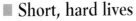

Bringing up the family

Female hominids gave birth every four to six years and suckled their babies for three to five years. The young remained with their mothers until they reached the age of 11. Then they learned to recognize the dangers in their environment, and to fend for themselves.

Short, hard lives

With a life expectancy as short as 20 years (compared with over 70 years now) and infant mortality of perhaps one in four (compared with one in 40 in western society today), life for our australopithecine ancestors was tough.

Fror

When our ancestors
abandoned life in the trees
they started making shelters
from branches.

■ Tree homes

Our primate ancestors had
closely-spaced and forward-
looking eyes that gave good
distance judgement for
jumping from branch to branch.
Their long arms and grasping hands
and feet were also well-adapted for
climbing and living in trees. Not only
were trees safe from predators on the
ground, but they also provided shelter
and food.

Stick-based shelter

■ Sheltering in the open

Early humans were not
so adept at climbing trees.
Between two and 1.5 million
years ago *Homo ergaster*
settled in areas where there
was little forest. They needed
shelter, and learned how to
build windproof huts out of
branches.

Cave

rees to Caves

■ The time of the caveman

Natural caves provided shelter but they were in
short supply. And early humans had to compete for
the caves with bears, lions and hyenas. Evidence of
cave occupation in China dates back 460,000 years.
In Europe, cave walls covered with paintings show
that generations of early modern humans lived in
them over a long period of time.

Mammoth bones and skins
were used for building
homes 40,000 years ago
in eastern Europe.

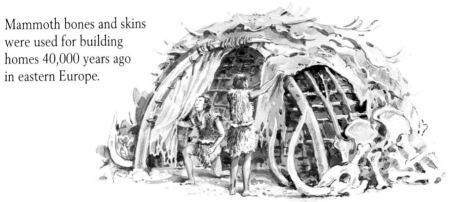

*Hut made of mammoth bones
and branches*

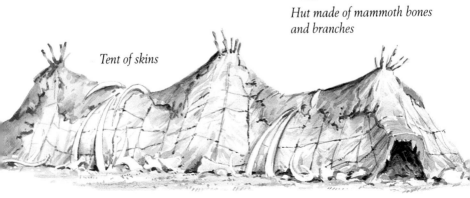

Tent of skins

In the south of France, right in the centre of Nice, the Terra Amata site was inhabited by people 380,000 years ago. On what was then a beach, ashes have been found, as well as elephant bones, deer antlers and stone tools. Excavation and study of the remains show that a large hut had been built from woven branches, propped up by a ring of stone blocks.

■ **To make a model hut indoors**

You will need:
- modelling clay or plasticine
- a sheet of card 20 x 30 cm
- small twigs of hazel or birch about 20 cm long
- some pebbles
- sand or earth for decoration

1. Roll out the clay to cover the card.
2. Stick two branches into the clay and prop them together as an entrance.
3. Place the other branches to form a conical hut.
4. Prop the twigs up with a circle of stones around the base.
5. To finish off, cover the clay with sand or earth.

mata Hut

You can also try making a life-sized hut outdoors.

■ **To make your Terra Amata hut**

You will need:
- forked hazel or birch branches 1.5–2 m in length
- rocks

1. Choose soft ground if possible. Start by pushing two branches into the ground (sharpening the ends will help). Tie them at the top to make an entrance.
2. Place a rock at the base of each branch.
3. Continue placing the branches as in the model.
4. Interweave any small side shoots and tie the top of the structure together.
5. Strengthen the base with more stones.
6. Now, sit inside and imagine what life was like all those years ago!

The Hunters and th

Most early hominids probably ate some meat, as some of the living apes do.

Killing a mammoth was a dangerous task.

Hunted

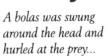

A bolas was swung around the head and hurled at the prey...

■ Safety in numbers

Early hunters wanted to get their food with the least risk to themselves and they worked together to achieve this. Small game such as deer, horses, birds and fish would have been their usual prey. However, there is evidence that dangerous animals such as elephants and mammoths were also hunted.

■ The hunters became the hunted

Some hominids were themselves hunted. The skull of a young australopithecine with cat tooth marks has been found in a South African cave. Around two million years ago, the cat dragged its victim by the head into its den.

...and the prey was snared by the thongs.

■ Sticks and stones

The oldest known wooden throwing spear dates back about 400,000 years. It was found in Germany with stone tools and the remains of a butchered horse. To kill such fast prey, hunters would have had to plan how to work together. This is the first good evidence of co-operative hunting for fresh meat by early modern humans.

■ Hi-tech hunting weapons

A 40,000-year-old blade-shaped killing stick, made of mammoth ivory, has been found in Poland. It was thrown like a boomerang to maim deer or wild cattle. Barbed harpoons, spear-throwers and bows and arrows were invented around 12,000 years ago. These weapons made it possible to hunt a greater variety of animals.

Tools and Techniques

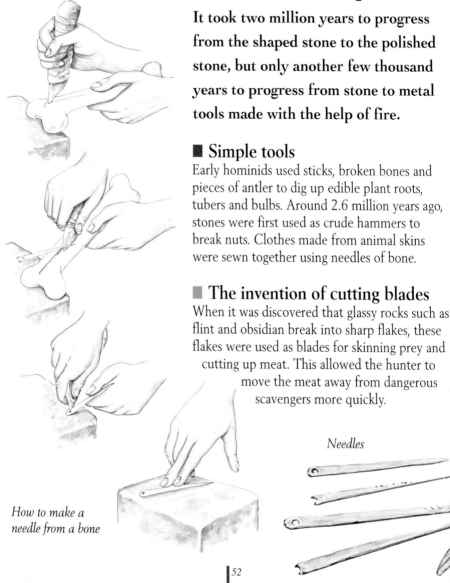

It took two million years to progress from the shaped stone to the polished stone, but only another few thousand years to progress from stone to metal tools made with the help of fire.

■ Simple tools

Early hominids used sticks, broken bones and pieces of antler to dig up edible plant roots, tubers and bulbs. Around 2.6 million years ago, stones were first used as crude hammers to break nuts. Clothes made from animal skins were sewn together using needles of bone.

■ The invention of cutting blades

When it was discovered that glassy rocks such as flint and obsidian break into sharp flakes, these flakes were used as blades for skinning prey and cutting up meat. This allowed the hunter to move the meat away from dangerous scavengers more quickly.

Needles

How to make a needle from a bone

Information

■ Better hand-axes

The invention of double-edged (bifacial) stone blades, around 1.4 million years ago, led to much more effective hand-axes. Axe-making sites have been found throughout Africa, Europe and Asia. Scattered fragments of stone are evidence of the original larger stones.

Skins for clothing were pierced with a sharp stone before being sewn together.

Speartips were tied to the wooden shaft with thin strips of leather and glued with resin.

Assegai tip

■ From stone to metal

Around 50,000 years ago, towards the end of the Ice Age, small razor-sharp stone flakes were used in weapons and in tools such as sickles. Stone arrow-heads were invented around 13,000 years ago. Making tools and weapons became a skilled craft, especially when agriculture began around 12,000 years ago. The first domestication of sheep and goats coincided with the use of fire to smelt copper metal for the first time, around 8,000 years ago.

Harpoons

Biface

Scraper

Chopper

Sliver of stone

Rock Art

Exactly why did our ancestors carve figurines and paint animals for more than 30,000 years? We can only guess.

This statuette of a woman is 25,000 years old.

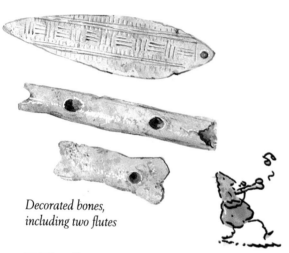

Decorated bones, including two flutes

▇ The first artists

Natural objects like shells were first used as jewellery by Neandertals about 50,000 years ago. Animals were carved on antlers, ivory and bones. They also featured in clay models and wall paintings. But portraits of humans are rare, apart from female figure carvings which might have some symbolic connection with childbirth.

54

■ Etched in stone

Engravings on stone survive better than paintings or bone carvings, so they are amongst the oldest preserved images. However, they are difficult to date.

Pigment is a paint or dye.

■ Talented Cro-Magnons

Wonderful rock art has been found all over the world. Painting began with the Cro-Magnons about 35,000 years ago. Coloured with natural *pigments*, the paintings show wild horses, herds of bison and other prey, as well as dangerous predators such as bears and lions. These vivid scenes help to take us back in time to the world of our prehistoric ancestors.

Our ancestors had only four main colours to work with, derived from natural pigments in soils and rocks. The most common colours (red, brown and yellow) are iron oxides. Black is manganese oxide, charcoal or soot. Use the same colours (in water-based paint) and try some Stone Age painting.

■ Charcoal drawing
Use a piece of barbecue (or artist's) charcoal to draw an animal outline. This is probably the oldest art material and it's still popular today.

A dab hand with swabs
Soak some moss (or cotton wool) in wet paint and decorate a pebble. Vary the amount of paint on the swab to give different textures.

■ Finger painting
Even chimps like doing this! See how many different kinds of lines you can make and how accurate you can be with paint-soaked fingers.

Stone Age Style

You will need:
- a green twig of hazel or birch (15cm long)
- a stone

■ Handprints

Pin a large piece of paper on a wall. Place one hand on the paper. Hold up a shallow dish of wet paint with the other hand and blow the paint at your hand. Be careful, this can be messy!

Crush and fray the end of the twig with the stone until you have a brush – then paint!

■ Mark your slate

Use a small piece of slate (or a modern nail, with care!) to draw on a bigger slate. If you make a mistake you can always wipe it off with a damp cloth, as Victorian school children did.

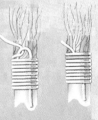

You can achieve the same effect by fraying one end of a 20-cm piece of string. Follow the four pictures above to tie it to a bamboo handle.

Most hominids are extinct.

True. Around one million years ago, as the world entered the Ice Age, several species of hominids became extinct, leaving only humans as survivors.

Humans are members of the ape family.

True We share a common ancestor with the apes.

Early humans spent all their time looking for food.

False. They had time to craft tools, paint pictures and look after the sick.

Language began at the time of the Cro-Magnons.

False. The necessity to communicate with language is linked to the first humans, such as Homo habilis.

Humans originated in Africa.

True. Modern humans all come from a group of hominids that originated in Africa 120,000 years ago.

Homo erectus knew of the yeti.

True. *Gigantopithecus*, the largest ape known (3 m tall and 540 kg in weight), lived at the same time in Southeast Asia and died out 500,000 years ago.

Our ancestors were brainier than us.

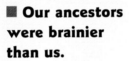

True. All early modern humans had bigger brains than us. But they also had bigger bodies, and brain size is related to body size.

Our prehistoric ancestors were cannibals.

Perhaps! Cut marks on the bones of early humans show that flesh was removed from the bodies — but we do not know what for.

Art is a Cro-Magnon invention.

True. Rock engravings, the oldest art, originated with the first Cro-Magnons.

■ Hominids took up walking to spot dangers lurking in the savannah grasslands.

■ Early humans were scavengers.

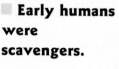

■ Lucy could sprint through the savannah.

■ Evolution stopp with the appearar of modern human

False. The early hominids were only about 1 m high and could not have seen over the tall grasses.

False. Although australopithecines like Lucy could walk upright, their leg joints did not allow them to run.

False. Evolution has no end and humans are only the most recent representatives of a huge family, the hominids.

■ Our prehistoric ancestors were cavemen.

True. They followed vultures to dead animals and hunted down small animals.

False. There are relatively few caves on Earth. Certainly they were used by our ancestors, but generally they built temporary shelters out of wood and skins.

■ Neandertals looked after the old and sick.

True. Burials of aged and infirm Neandertals show that they must have been cared for to have survived as long as they did.

■ Cro-Magnons killed off the Neandertals.

False. The Neandertals slowly died out at different times in different places. Our ancestors do not appear to have interbred with them.

Index

Africa 14, 15, 20, 21, 22, 23, 28, 30, 36, 37, 42, 51, 59
America 14
ape 14, 16-17, 19, 20, 38, 45, 50, 58
archaeologist 34, 35
art 31, 37, 47, 54-55, 59
Asia 14, 15, 26, 30, 59
Australopithecine 12, 13, 20, 21, 22-23, 24, 25, 37, 38, 39, 42, 45, 51, 60
Australopithecus afarensis 13, 23
Australopithecus africanus 13, 37
Australopithecus anamensis 13, 23, 39
Australopithecus bahrelghazali 13
Australopithecus ramidus 13
Australopithecus robustus 13
axe 26, 27, 53

boomerang 51
building 31, 46-47, 61

burial 29, 31, 61

cannibalism 59
chimpanzee 14, 17, 24
China 27, 36, 47
climate 19, 24, 26
clothes 52
Cro-Magnon 12, 30, 31, 39, 55, 58, 59, 61

Darwin, Charles 16
dinosaur 19

Europe 14, 26, 28, 29
evolution 18-19, 60

fire 27, 35, 40-41, 42, 43, 52
food 23, 40, 41, 42-43, 50, 51, 52
France 27
fossil 20, 23, 27, 34, 35, 38, 39

gene 16, 18, 30
geochemist 34
geologist 34
Germany 51
Gigantopithecus 59
goat 53
gorilla 13, 17, 24

hominid 12, 14, 15, 20, 21, 24, 25, 26, 30, 35, 38, 39, 40, 41, 42, 44, 45, 50, 51, 58, 60
Homo erectus 13, 27, 28, 39
Homo ergaster 46
Homo habilis 13, 38, 24, 25, 58
Homo rudolfensis 13, 25
Homo sapiens 12, 13, 30
hunting 23, 29, 50-51, 61

Ice Age 28, 29, 58

Java 27
jewellery 54

knuckle-walking 22

Laetoli footprints 36, 39
language 27, 45, 58
Leakey, Louis, Mary and Richard 36
Lucy 22, 60

mammoth 47
metal 53
music 29

Neandertal 12, 28-29, 30, 31, 39, 61
needle 52

painting 31, 37, 47, 54-55
palaeo-anthropologist 34
palaeontologist 34
palynologist 34
paranthrope 12, 24
Poland 51

Rift Valley 20, 21, 22, 23, 35, 36

sculpture 54-55
sedimentologist 34
sickle 53
sheep 53
spear 30, 31, 51, 53

Taung child 37
tools 14, 15, 17, 24, 25, 26, 31, 34, 35, 51, 52-3

Solution to the game on pages 32-33

should have found the inscription 'Post No Bills' (which first appeared on July 29, 1881), the dinosaur (dinosaurs were extinct before humans appeared), the feeding bottle (19th century), the stamped letter (1820), the pteranodon (like the dinosaurs, nct), the dressmaker's tape measure (18th century), the pair of scissors (17th century), the woman knitting (AD 200), the watch n century), the spectacles (18th century), the book (in 1447, Gutenberg printed the first books), the hoop (this toy originated in ient Greece), the lighter (modern), the cooking pot (the first known pots are Neolithic), the sword (lst century AD), the pyramid first pyramids were built by the Egyptians 4,000 years ago), the field of corn (Neolithic), the herd of cows (Neolithic), the tent s (20th century).

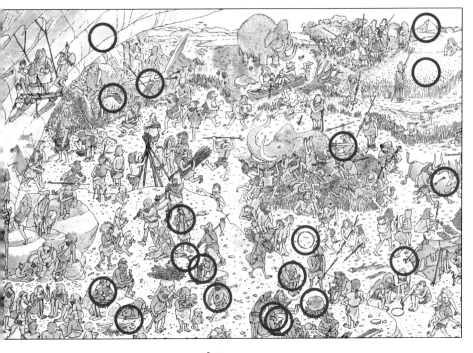

Created by Marie-Odile Fordacq
Authors Jean-Loup Craipeau, Béatrice Garel, Catherine Pauwels, Pascal Picq
Managing editors Marie-Odile Fordacq, Camilla Hallinan
Editorial co-ordinators Ariane Léandri, Molly Perham
Art editors Sue Aldworth, Ch'en Ling, Bernard Girodroux, Val Pidgeon
Illustrators Ian Chamberlain, Jeff Fisher, Chris Forsey, Daniel Guerrier, Nick Hall,
Christian Hook, Ruth Lindsay, Richard Ward, Philippe Werner
Activities Ting Morris, Tim Ridley Photography, Val Wright
Photo research Veneta Bullen
Photo credits B & C Alexander, Ancient Art & Architecture Collection, Bruce Coleman,
Frank Lane Picture Agency, Natural History Museum, NHPA, Oxford Scientific Films,
Planet Earth Pictures, The Stockmarket / Zefa
Design and page make-up équipage, Olivier Lemoine,
Judy Linard, Terry Woodley

KINGFISHER
An imprint of Kingfisher Publications Plc
New Penderel House, 283–288 High Holborn, London WC1V 7HZ

This edition first published by Kingfisher Publications Plc 1998
Originally published in France by Nathan
under the title *Megascope: à la rencontre des hommes préhistorques*

2 4 6 8 10 9 7 5 3 1

A CIP catalogue record for this book is available
from the British Library

ISBN 07534 0 225 4

Printed in Italy

Stickers

Skull of *Australopithecus robustus*, 2 million years BC. (Tanzania)

Skull of the Taung Child, 2 million years BC. (South Africa)

Skull of *Homo erectus* ('Peking Man'), 300,000 years BC.

A grinding stone, 1.7 million years old. (East Africa)

Biface made of black flint, 40,000 to 55,000 years BC. (Moustier, France)

Sharpened tool, 40,000 years BC.

Sculpture of a bison and horse, about 20,000 years BC. (Abri de Roc-de-Sers, France)

Laurel leaf, 44,000 to 33,000 years BC.

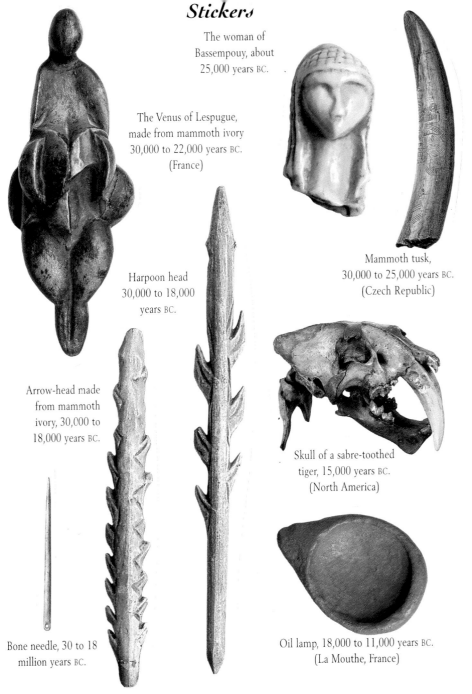

Stickers

The woman of Bassempouy, about 25,000 years BC.

The Venus of Lespugue, made from mammoth ivory 30,000 to 22,000 years BC. (France)

Mammoth tusk, 30,000 to 25,000 years BC. (Czech Republic)

Harpoon head 30,000 to 18,000 years BC.

Arrow-head made from mammoth ivory, 30,000 to 18,000 years BC.

Skull of a sabre-toothed tiger, 15,000 years BC. (North America)

Bone needle, 30 to 18 million years BC.

Oil lamp, 18,000 to 11,000 years BC. (La Mouthe, France)